Citizens

Citizens
Ian Parks

Smokestack Books
1 Lake Terrace, Grewelthorpe, Ripon HG4 3BU
e-mail: info@smokestack-books.co.uk
www.smokestack-books.co.uk

Text copyright 2017, Ian Parks, all rights reserved.

ISBN 978-0-9955635-6-8

Smokestack Books is
represented
by Inpress Ltd

for Steve Ely

'*There was at least somewhere
where revolutionary memory
could persist*'
Simon Schama

Contents

Citizens	11
The Thread	12
Since	13
Oracle	14
Towpath	16
Registry of Births and Deaths	17
Wootton Bassett	18
Honeyboy Edwards	19
The Bowl	20
Beach Hut	21
Snooker	23
Allotments	24
Gladstone's Axe	25
Spa	26
The Levellers	27
Glitter Ball	28
Strike Breakers	29
Paragon	31
Ellis Island	32
The Land of Green Ginger	33
Cat and Man	35
Ella	36
Stormbringer	42
Burne-Jones Window	43
A Bricked-up Window on the Great North Road	44
Road Block	45
Mainland	46
Laura	47
A Tree Grows through the Ruins of a House	48
The Arrow Slit	49
Harmonica	50

Harlech and Beyond	51
The Tango	52
House of Cards	53
Shakespeare's Lovers	54
New Year	55
Metro	56
Iron Hague	57
Cable Street	58
Learning the Blues	59
Chantry Bridge	61
Queen's Square	62
Bloody Meadows	63
Ice	64
Elegy for the Chartist Poets	65

Citizens

Free agents, this is how we made our way,
our used car swerving through the new estates.
It was late springtime and the fields of oil-seed rape

flashed out their yellow signal to the sky.
We travelled incognito and we didn't cast a vote.
Night found us parked up on some empty beach

to watch the moon come clear and fade.
The European flag was everywhere – twelve stars
encircling nothing on a ground of midnight blue.

The cities had no feature and the landscape had no soul.
Girls waved from the corner as we hit the open road,
our every exit covered by a camera on a pole.

The Thread

I sit beside the fire and watch you knit –
the click of needles as the embers burn,
the silent counting underneath the breath –
and find myself absorbed in it.

More than anything that might be done or said
between the acts of going and return
to this old building that I've come to love
the ravelling of purple, black, and red

as you pause and slip and purl inside the loop.
So weave a hair from your inclining head
into the fabric where you sit
to bind me closer to you when I go.

Through the long months of rain and ice
and floods and falling snow
the narrative of us and what we did:
all your lost generations in the thread.

Citizens

Free agents, this is how we made our way,
our used car swerving through the new estates.
It was late springtime and the fields of oil-seed rape

flashed out their yellow signal to the sky.
We travelled incognito and we didn't cast a vote.
Night found us parked up on some empty beach

to watch the moon come clear and fade.
The European flag was everywhere – twelve stars
encircling nothing on a ground of midnight blue.

The cities had no feature and the landscape had no soul.
Girls waved from the corner as we hit the open road,
our every exit covered by a camera on a pole.

The Thread

I sit beside the fire and watch you knit –
the click of needles as the embers burn,
the silent counting underneath the breath –
and find myself absorbed in it.

More than anything that might be done or said
between the acts of going and return
to this old building that I've come to love
the ravelling of purple, black, and red

as you pause and slip and purl inside the loop.
So weave a hair from your inclining head
into the fabric where you sit
to bind me closer to you when I go.

Through the long months of rain and ice
and floods and falling snow
the narrative of us and what we did:
all your lost generations in the thread.

Since

Since then I've crossed a flooded continent
and dreamt a better ending: one in which
the door was never opened, never closed;
where the false intelligence was never sent
and the road not taken was the taken road.
Since then I've found another way
of saying all the things I should have said
about the impulse and the laws imposed;
the freedoms we once had and where they went.

Oracle

I had a question for her so I went
through convoluted alleys to the place:
no sacred grove of olives but a mill
abandoned when the textiles died.

Reached by a narrow staircase
with a missing step, the top floor
opened to the sky, exposed.
Each city has an underside –

a burnt-out region to avoid
where streets are unlit and no one goes.
And there I found her,
cold and drugged and shivering

on the mattress where she dozed.
Not as old as you'd expect
for someone so acquainted with the world,
when she reached her hand out

and the moonlight fell on it
there were no wrinkles puckering the skin.
I gave her nothing but a crumpled note.
She cast her glass beads on the floor.

Her answer came in riddles
as if what I'd asked her were no easy thing
but a question with no answer
and no language left for it.

Escape was easier than I'd thought.
I needed no direction and no guide.
Instinct led me to the upper air.
I climbed onto the rooftops

and looked out: the spires
and domes and minarets
reclaiming their identity from night,
the dawn a yellow slit.

Towpath

Another time I'll take you to the pub
where old men spend all day over one pint.
For now we have the towpath laced with frost –

the things I won't admit to in my heart,
the ritual dying of the winter sun.
You'd never think the hill across the way

was once a slagheap – useless, overgrown
where three untethered horses graze,
cropping the shallow-rooted grass -

just as I'd never venture to explain
the wide canal that cuts under it all,
the things it once displaced.

So claim this morning as your own.
Choose your moment. Time it well.
Unleash the dogs and watch them run.

Registry of Births and Deaths

They queued for hours outside my door
to register the deaths of men –
of husbands, fathers, brothers, sons
who died in some disaster underground:
crushed when seams collapsed, encasing them
or choked inhaling poisonous fumes.

My front from used to be the office where
those girls and women in grey shawls
offered small comfort, held back tears,
a drop of ink and scraping pen
reducing flesh and blood to dates and names,
of infants also, born to coal and dust;

the deaths of them, the deep successive tides.
At night I blink back darkness from my bed,
lie sleepless listening to the timeless air.
The town itself is riddled and subsides,
the barefoot shuffling of their feet
a tremor running through the downstairs rooms.

Wootton Bassett

There are no theories to explain
what happens when a country goes to war.
Poppies hide behind their crimson screen –

hedgerows falter, disappear,
horses stir, turned out to grass
and everything that England means

or might mean to a stranger standing here
is contained and diminished
to a row of shining cars,

streets lined and silent, flowers thrown;
the flag-draped coffins as they pass
through Wootton Bassett in the rain.

Honeyboy Edwards

No one played the blues like Honeyboy.
I heard him once in Sheffield
when he was at his best.
The delta mud had baked him dry,
depositing its silt like coffee grains

under his scalp, his fingernails,
run like high water in the night
through Vicksburg and Helena
and sifted through his veins.
You saw it when he lifted up his head

as if the notes were in the sky
and when he smiled at something
only he could understand –
some chord reached for, almost missed,
learned from a bluesman

when he was a child, the hard quicksilver
those twelve bars imposed –
that he was the last of his kind.
That's why I tried to set it down;
the still air undisturbed by a gold fan,

the beginning and the sudden end
of songs I only heard just once,
the calluses that numbed his fingertips.
There were things to look at
in the crowded room: the girls

short-skirted and high-heeled,
the faces of the ones who'd come
to try to read his mind
but Honeyboy was ninety
and his eyes were closed.

The Bowl

I never think of visiting
her grave – she isn't there.
Instead I take her favourite fruit

and place it in a bowl,
examining each crimson fleck
until the impulse fades.

In Athens once I came across
a beggar with no eyes,
making a shallow cradle

with his hands; his hands
containing nothing but the air.
I stare and think of nothing.

If the cradling hands
are the will to life
the bruised fruit is the soul.

Beach Hut

It's thirty years since I undid the lock
to spend a rented summer under glass –
a space no bigger than my bedroom now,
the skylight slanting, sunlight through the planks.

Blue meant a day for swimming in the sea;
grey for reading till the weather cleared.
One room where everything I needed was to hand:
bare floorboards, faded rug, sand in my hair

and in my jeans. It was a year of rioting,
of running battles through the city streets,
of looted shop-fronts, shattered glass,
cars overturned and burning in the road.

The rumour of it didn't reach me there.
I spread my sheets, slept on the floor,
hung a rusted oil-lamp from a beam,
convinced the answer could be found

in solitude and in the distant sound
of waves as they came crashing to the shore.
The place was a ramshackle wreck
held up by a lick of yellow paint.

At night a big ship loomed against the sky
and from its bright and polished deck
someone I imagined lit a foreign cigarette
and smoked it slowly, leaning from the rail.

Just once I saw a torchlight flashing back.
But mostly it was dunes, resilient grass,
the dog-eared books I read then threw away –
the narratives I didn't want to share.

The days grew shorter. Cold set in.
The beach huts emptied. I grew bored.
Rain drove in every morning from the sea.
I packed my rucksack, caught a train,

sped through a landscape changed
to find the world not waiting anymore,
back to the city with its new façade
and the headlines I'd ignored.

Snooker

I learned to play it in the dim-lit halls
or in the backrooms of disreputable pubs
where women we were warned about would go
to sit on barstools, showing off their legs.

A coin in the meter bought us an hour
away from homework in the smoky haze
that spread across the table where we played.
Our elders and our betters disapproved,

seeing in the free balls and the four-aways
the surest sign of a misspent youth.
We should be doing paper rounds or sleeping in our beds.
I was drawn to the white ball swerving,

the gentle thud of ivory on green baize,
the blue chalk powdering our clothes.
There's no money in it my grandfather said,
which was his way of telling me

that writing poetry had no money in it too.
John Spencer and Ray Reardon held their cues
in photographs that lined the woodchip walls
or smiled at us with trophies in their hands.

The men who taught me how to play are dead;
their sons prefer computer games and pool.
I found a kind of truth in it and often do –
the unlooked for soft collisions, reds kissing reds.

Allotments

Their wives would never think of visiting
these bent ramshackle sheds
made out of doors and windowpanes
where the loose tarpaulin flaps

and if the paint is flaking it can flake.
Inside a scattering of faded rugs,
horsehair chairs, the tang of paraffin.
A yellow pile of *The South Yorkshire Times*

is topped by a flask and a white enamel mug.
Green shoots invade the stubborn soil.
The young don't want them and the old
have given up on leeks and radishes.

And so the men who used to work the pits
take on these narrow strips – a hinterland
of tubs and greenhouses, slanting frames;
coax life from coal dust and a sprinkling

of water from a rusted can. Sunset is their hour:
it's then you'll find them on the far side of the hill,
talking sport and politics, scanning the rooftops, whistling
and waiting for their pigeons to come home.

Gladstone's Axe

Something apocalyptic in the way
he took it to the root of everything,
striding the grounds of his Welsh estate
impervious to the rain and felling trees.
He solved the Irish Question between blows,
the last trunk creaking, crashing down

when he was in his eighties, close to death.
The statues and the paths are overgrown.
It's in the room below me where I sleep.
On rain-dark mornings such as these
when all I hear are misused words
like *freedom*, *trust*, *austerity*

I want to break the intervening glass,
remove it from its velvet case,
grip it tightly with both hands
and without reverence or restraint
go out into the waiting world
and do some felling of my own.

Spa

It must be all of forty years
and still I think I've found the exact spot:
the spa the colour of wet sand

and rock pools strewn with bladderwrack.
An ice-cream leaks into the crevice of my hand.
I pick my way among the rocks,

the giant pebbles bleached and pocked.
This is where my parents stopped to kiss –
a quintet playing thirties jazz,

old men on faded deckchairs listening –
my mother flustered as I turned to look.
The spa is held in place by scaffolding.

I blink at the sun and shade my eyes.
There are no landmarks on this empty beach
There is no safe way back.

The Levellers

More radical than Cromwell, more extreme,
he had them lined against the wall and shot
in Burford where he tracked them down.
If there were any final words

those words have not survived.
Silence commemorates a state of mind,
an instinct born sharp-edged in civil war.
Once started, where does revolution stop?

You kill the king but who picks up his crown?
They wanted a changed world
where everything was equal, levelled out –
debated what it meant and died for it.

The axe is at the root of everything,
the articles are nailed upon the door.
In cramped, oak-panelled rooms
down tangled alleys, up twisting stairs

they spread their map of freedom out,
hung lamps from beams and leaned into
their dangerous words, their hushed conspiracies.
Each year, around the churchyard

where they fell, we come to celebrate:
beer-tents, loud music, four-by-fours,
the trappings of our new-found affluence;
the clamouring of children wanting more.

Glitter Ball

The dance floor's empty but for us.
We shuffle to a solo saxophone.
The decade flickers and goes out.
Our wedding day is over now
and still you find it possible to rest
your temple on my shoulder as we sway.
The glitter ball is spinning overhead,

dispersing light and swivelling
into the corners of the room
where guests are lingering, staying on.
The memory flashes now you're gone –
lights up the mirrors, bounces back
from ceilings, faces, tables, walls:
sharp, fragmented, faceted.

Strike Breakers

Look at them now. Who'd think that once
they braved the picket line?
Sitting at the far end of the bar,
ignored by those who went on strike
they spend all afternoon over one pint

or stare down at the carpet's threadbare swirls.
In this pit village memory is long –
as long as shadows that extend
the full length of the valley
from the miner's welfare to the cenotaph.

The room is crowded with the young:
the brash call centre workers and their girls.
Whatever else they might have done –
rescued a neighbour from a flooded seam
or pulled a man to safety

when the props gave way
is forgotten and means nothing, counts for less.
They went back before they were allowed.
While others scraped the slag-heap
for a bucket full of coal

or held the line at Orgreave
when the mounted men broke through
they thought about their families, drifted back,
were ferried under escort
to the pit head by police.

They weren't there when the brass bands played
and banners were unfurled,
when the men marched to the pit gate
as if they'd won the day.
They weren't there when the promises were made.

Remembered for one thing they pass the time.
They want to be forgiven but we can't forgive.
The seam runs deep and deeper than you'd think.
These are the cards that are dealt to us
and this is the life we live.

Paragon

The longest platform in the world.
We walked its length together in the rain
impervious to the masses gathered there.
Each plate-glass window trapped a thin-lipped ghost

suspended high above us where we stood
among the rafters open to the night.
Their warnings went unheard.
We brushed the scarves and overcoats

of huddled immigrants, their eyes
fixed on the promise of a distant continent.
All the generations, everything they owned
strapped tight inside a worn suitcase.

Not the silent waiting but the journey back:
the steam-flanked train accelerating,
your lips a flash of scarlet and your face
reflected in the glass. The estuary exuding milky light.

Ellis Island

Departing or arriving
what they leave here are their names,
the last of empire clinging on.
Disembarking on the landing stage
the first thing that they learn
is how to shed their other lives –
the Jolsons, Gershwins, and Berlins
and those we've never heard of too
discovering that freedom
is not a given right
but something they must earn.
On wharves and in the harbour bars
the immigrant songs unsung.
In the middle of this picture
picture me: the one
you wouldn't look at twice
scanning the skyline silently.
Birds on the tide-line quarrelling,
light pin-pricked across the waves
from each tall edifice.
Out in the harbour Liberty
and in her tight-clenched fist
a torch that doesn't burn.

The Land of Green Ginger

Here is the smallest window
in the world. Look through it
squinting with one eye.
You'll see the things
you're not supposed to see:
the politician cheating

on his wife, the fat priest
stealing from the poor,
the poet scribbling
someone else's lines.
Only in this quarter,
in this district of the town

and only through this green
and stamp-sized frame
that didn't shatter in the blitz
can you expect to see
things as they really are.
Other windows hide from us,

distract us and distort.
But this is the Land
of Green Ginger –
a place where the sky
and the estuary meet;
where all the thin alleys

deceive, double back
and lead to a spot
where strangeness occurs.
Put your eye to the window,
see how England goes;
its coalitions and its wars,

the steady consolation
of the rain, the failure
to respond or change
its constitutions or its laws.
Once I drank bitter
from a clouded glass

among the city's dissident
and peered out later
on the green-tinged street
where the world
of commerce came and went,
their ebb and flow

refracted and contained
inside the confines
of a thick glass pane.
The barmaid blinked
a tear back from her eye.
Then, after drinking,

I went out into the bright
unequivocal day,
arrived too early or too late.
For this is the Land
of Green Ginger
and this is the window

that never lies –
where looking just once
means looking again
at what you think you know
of this city of lost chances
where the rail lines terminate.

Cat and Man

The story as I heard it went like this:
a knight was riding home from the crusades
when something fell and fastened on his neck –
a wildcat waiting in the woods
that dropped so sudden, screeched so loud

the knight's horse reared and bolted at the shock.
In the mile between the ambush
and the safety of the church
he fought a running battle, dripping blood.
The cat would slink off then come back.

Next morning, when they found him in the porch
the stricken man had stiffened as he died,
crushing the cat against the sandstone wall.
They buried them together as you would,
raising a wooden effigy to mark the spot.

I edged in from the sunlight as a child.
Scaffolding was holding up the spire.
Six hundred years had passed and still
the bloodstains deepened on the flags.
The knight was very dead, his hands

were pressed together as he prayed.
The cat still had some life in him.
He looked as if he'd wake up with a snarl,
spring through the windows of the nearby pub
where the drinking locals told a different tale.

Ella

1

The only thing we had in common was our love of jazz. On Friday nights my father would come home from the pit, coal dust rimming his eyes, take a shellac 78 from the stack, slip it from its faded paper sleeve, and place it on the turntable. He always started with Ella and he always finished with her too. There was something in her optimism, the purity of her tone, her immaculate diction, the phrasing and her choice of material that attracted him. And there we would sit, father and son, tapping our feet and drinking our tea to sounds that had been made at the other side of the Atlantic, in another time, another world. We never talked. All we did was listen, exchange knowing nods when Ella reached a particularly sublime note or when she'd launch into one of those wordless, improvised flights – the scatting she was so famous for. A silent complicity passed between us then. The looks we exchanged expressed approval for the favourites he would always play. He'd put his head back, cup his hands around the back of it, close his eyes and hum. The purple coal scar on his wrist throbbed slightly as he sang.

I can never remember where my mother was or what part she played in all of this – in the kitchen cooking supper probably, or doing the ironing upstairs. There were no photos of Ella on the record sleeves. Because I'd never seen her, Ella could be anyone I wanted her to be – and I wanted her to be a slender blonde in a slinky satin dress, leaning against the piano as she sang. We each had songs that held a special significance for us. I liked *If I Could Write a Book,* my father *My Heart Stood Still* but we both loved *Manhattan* with its promise of New York, Central Park, the Bronx and Staten Island too, the hydrants spurting jets, heat escaping from the subway. I was never allowed to touch the records. The rest of the time it was indifference, hostility even: a deliberate, calculated avoidance of each other made difficult by the smallness of the terrace house we shared. My father was rarely there. Sometimes, when he was working awkward shifts, we wouldn't see each other for days on end. Every night, seven nights a week, he'd go out drinking in the working men's clubs to laugh, and smoke, to place bets on the horses with the other miners and to shine. He was a singer too. A thread connecting him directly to Ella and to Frank.

On Saturday nights I would go out with him. One time it would be the Miner's Arms, another time the Main Street Club. He'd do it for nothing, or for free beer, or a used fiver. For the love of the music, he would say. Had he not got married and had me, he pointed out, he could have turned professional, done it for a living. Then there was the applause. He had a way with a song – leaning into the microphone, eyes half-closed, his black quiff falling into his eyes, keeping time with a click of his finger and his thumb, a certain intensity. He didn't sing a song. He embraced it. He knew, as Ella and Frank and Billie and Dean all knew, that if you understood the story you understood the song. A little drama, perfect, self-contained. And if you understood it then the audience would understand it too whether they were the well-heeled crowd at the Sands Hotel or the wives of miners on port and lemon, lager and lime. He was the sort you'd take the wife to see: a crooner, a charmer, as slick as you could ever hope to get in a bleak South Yorkshire mining town. 'This one', he would say, 'is for all you ladies out there' and he'd nod to the organist who started to play. He'd open with *Witchcraft* and end with *As Time Goes By*. Standards. The story and the song. I would sit there with my half of shandy and packet of crisps. I was drawn in too. Everyone remembers the strike in the middle of the eighties: Orgreave, flying pickets, road blocks, Scargill, scabs, the shame of defeat. But ten years earlier there'd been another strike – the one that's forgotten about - and the miners had won. They had a bit of money in their pockets. Some of them spent it on a new motorbike or a holiday abroad or taking the wife to see turns. My father spent it on going to see Ella.

The first thing I knew about it was on one of those Friday nights. The coal had just been delivered: a huge mound piled up outside the front door and outside every other front door in the street.

It was always my job to 'get it in' – to shovel the whole ton of it down the grate and into the cellar before I had my tea. You were looked down on by the neighbours if you didn't get the coal in on the day that it arrived. 'Here's some spending money', my mother had said. 'Your Dad's taking you to London tomorrow. You're going to see Ella'. There had been an argument. My dad was edgy, silent, volatile, biting his nails, counting the minutes to seven o'clock when he could go out and become someone else. Not long before he'd pulled one of his mates out from under a pile of 'muck' – the pitman's word for rock and rubble – when the props had given way. His mate had shuddered and stared and died. He didn't talk about it but my mother would silence my questions with a look and a shaking of her head.

2

There was the warm whoosh of the underground, my father confused as I was in an unfamiliar world. We were staying in a cheap bed and breakfast in Holloway, a stone's throw from the women's prison which you could see from the window of the attic room we shared. I kept thinking of Ruth Ellis, shivering, waiting to be hung. 'They ought to build a lot more of them', my dad had said, laughing at his own joke. My mum and dad had been in London before – on their honeymoon – but this was my first time. I knew all the stories of course: how they'd danced into the early hours to Victor Silvester and how my dad was taken in for questioning by two plain-clothes policemen as they came out of the tube at Russell Square because he fitted the description of someone who'd killed a woman in her Kensington flat and because he was wearing the same sort of overcoat. The murderer had a Yorkshire accent too. I lay on the bed while my father shaved. 'Watch me', he said, 'you might learn something'. Steam rising from the chipped basin, a thick creamy lather, his face distorted in the oval mirror as the razor slid over his cheeks, the patting dry, the stringent tang of aftershave. Afterwards he rummaged in his bag. 'You'll be needing this', he said, and handed me a tie already tied, a loop to put over my head.

3

The tie is uncomfortable and doesn't go with my shirt. Purple and yellow don't match. The club is crowded and smaller than I'd expected. Intimate, as I'd later learn to say. Instead of seats in rows there are small round tables and on the tables tablecloths with candles in bottles and green glass ashtrays. My dad is disappointed because they don't serve beer. The walls are lined with signed photographs of all the greats who'd played here before. I don't know most of them. My dad is wearing his best suit but looks uneasy, out of place, conspicuous among the black polo necks, the tweed jackets and goatees. For them jazz is something to be discussed and understood; not something to love, respond to instinctively. Our table is right at the front. 'Good seats', my dad says loudly. I'm the youngest person in the room. The smoke encloses me and closes in. There's a murmur, a ripple, then a hush. Even my dad's cigarettes stand out: he smokes Capstain's Full Strength while the others are puffing on Camels, making a gesture out of every draw and blow. Nothing passes between my dad and me although I feel him there more powerfully than ever before, an acute awareness of his otherness as he plays with his wedding ring and taps the table top.

There's no fuss, no announcement. The lights go down and a black man in a tuxedo comes on stage and sits at the piano as if it's him we've come to see; another takes up a double bass. They run through a couple of notes then sidle into a number I try hard to place but can't. Then Ella makes her appearance. Her dress, as my dad would later say, 'fits where it touches', she wears her wig as nonchalantly as she'd wear a hat. It looks as if she'd grabbed it at the last minute as an afterthought, placing it on her head between the dressing room and the stage, never checked it in the mirror. Her glasses – 'thick as jam-jar bottoms' as my dad would also later say – magnify her half-closed eyes, her lashes quivering. She surveys the audience for a few seconds. She senses my attention. She looks at me and smiles. And as she smiles she sings.

Someday he'll come along, the man I love

Everyone who was looking at Ella is now looking at me. I'm trying to smile back and find I'm smiling at my shoes. She's squinting in the spotlight. Ira's words are slipping through. Intently, deliberately, in a soft-and-measured, inexplicable way the lyrics reach for and touch a deep uncertain part of me.

And he'll be big and strong, the man I love

I'm neither big nor strong. I'm skinny fourteen. I don't want to follow my father down the pit. He doesn't know this yet and I don't know how I'm going to tell him. All I know are the drawn-out syllables, the modulation, the casual slide from one note to another, the secret of the story and the song. And now the bass is throbbing gently too, climbing and descending as she sings.

He'll build a little home, just meant for two

I'm thinking of my mother thinking of me. How she would have loved to have been there and how the story of it would soon enter the story of her life which was, in itself, a series of songs; my embarrassment, Ella's refusal to break the gaze, the audience loving it, wanting more. 'Your father loves you', she would say when he was out, 'but he doesn't know how to show it'. Perhaps he was showing it now.

From which he'd never roam, who would, would you?

How, I'm wondering, could Ella and my father exist in the same world? And how could it be that they are just a few feet apart with only me between them, breathing in the same swirling, smoke-filled air? How could those disparate lives meet and mesh in this enclosed space, this point in time, in this particular song? She squints again and her squint is endearing. The softness draws me to her. The singer and the story and the song.

And so all else above, I'm looking for the man I love

The song ends and everyone applauds. I find myself applauding too. But it's not the sort of applause I'm used to – the raucous spontaneous applause my father gets on a Saturday night – but an appreciative, restrained and knowing ripple starting at the stage and spreading out to the edges. The watch on my wrist stops ticking and will never go again. Ella's earrings catch the yellow light. She's hardly started and her forehead glistens and glows. She mops it with a pink silk handkerchief, takes a stiff and awkward bow and then launches into something else. Ellington. Although I try to catch her eye all night she never looks at me again.

4

The rain came against the window. London rain. It blurred the amber streetlights. We lay there in the darkness on our narrow, springless beds. I could hear my father humming, humming, humming. 'We won't forget this, will we?', he said, 'whatever else happens, we won't forget.' I pretended to be asleep. He turned over on his side and from under the covers I could hear the sound of weeping.

Stormbringer

The storm inflicts its damage and moves on –
a revolution in the night, a wave about to break.

Avenging angel, tearing up the street,
alive inside the thunder and the driving rain –

the lightning strike disrupting everything:
strafing the glass, uprooting trees,

bringing down this fragile house of cards,
the firstborn restless in their beds.

A tense reverberation in the brain;
the wide-eyed dead sprawled awkward in its wake.

Burne-Jones Window

We stood together in the nave.
You slipped your hand in my hand secretly
and with the other pointed out
the hidden secrets of the place:

the corners and recesses
filled with purple light
and all the things you wanted me to see.
I was so lost with love for you

I failed to catch the radiance
you showed: the stillness
at the heart of that nativity –
the virgin's head inclining to the child,

Joseph absent, somewhere else,
the slightly awkward reverence
of the shepherds and the kings,
the watery sunlight as it fell

and all of it enclosed:
a canopy of green, unfolded wings.
There were fresh flowers on a new-dug grave.
If you were to ask me what I took

from that brief interlude it would be this:
that the winter was suspended
in the fragile, coloured glass
and all the silent angels had your face.

A Bricked-up Window on the Great North Road

She drives too fast but always slows to see
a bricked up window on the Great North Road.
She says it used to make her think of me
and now it makes her think of politics –

of how a government can stretch its arm
as far as air and sunlight which are free.
I think it has no meaning: except that bricks
and mortar fill a space where choices used to be.

Road Block

The policeman in the middle of the road
isn't from here. Raising his hand
to flag us to one side, his accent placed him
somewhere further south. My father swears
and winds the window down.
An early morning rain stipples the screen
and through it, just, we start to see
the black and yellow barrier put in place
to keep us from the country lane
that leads out to the coking plant
is lifting slow, reluctantly.
We walked it freely in the months before the strike
but the trees are bare and the birds are gone.
Six of us are crowded in the back:
a big shaved-headed miner is sitting on my knee.
The officer is young and trembling.
He wants to know what brought us here
in the hour before the milk floats stir
when the innocent are turning in their beds
and only flying pickets and those up to no good
would make this turn. He wants to know
our names and where we're going after this.
Rain drips from his helmet as he waits for our reply.
We tell him *Monte Carlo* and drive on.

Mainland

After the chat shows and the bulletins,
the forecasts and the late reviews
I trim the oil-lamp, clear a space
and take one final look across the straits.
I came here to escape a darkening world.

Why should I listen to its news?
The mainland is a purple smudge;
the sea so shallow and so calm
you'd think that you could walk across
instead of waiting for the week it takes

before the ferry makes the harbour mouth
bringing cards and letters, word from home.
There's nothing but a mile
of dry-stone walls and unrelenting rain
between this cottage and the nearest farm

hidden by the intervening ridge.
Suspended here, the moment waits
still stranded in another century
when news was a fast as a gasping horse
and last year's revolution still to come.

Laura

This is the poem I promised you
on the night train where we met.
You were a stranger passing through
a landscape since grown derelict –
the towns and cities I once knew
before the furnaces went out.
A tune was running through my head,
the score of an old film
I'd seen but then forgot –
a film in which a girl is pronounced dead

but comes back in the final reel
to mesmerise the hero with her smile.
Of course it wasn't Hollywood
but Sheffield with its torn-out heart,
the steel works and the factories
long gone. But it was where
I used to queue to see
those plots unfolding on the screen.
I started whistling the theme

and you, the girl I'd never met,
joined in as we lurched
and swerved and slowed.
The memory starts to fade
and I begin to doubt it
I lean to lip-read through the glass.
I'm Laura you mouthed
as the train pulled out
and the drizzle turned to steam.
Laura's my name. I'm telling you this
in case you want to write about it.

A Tree Grows through the Ruins of a House

Each morning on my way
to watch a loved one die
I stop and look at what
the tree has done:
its roots disrupt foundations,
bring them down; its branches
intersect the summer sky.

What was a house
is now a crumbling shell,
becoming something other
than the thing it used to be –
completely overtaken by the green.

You have to reconstruct
each door and window frame,
imagine structures
where four walls have been.

The tree puts out its shoots.
Invisible, unseen,
the will to life persisting
in among the fallen stone.

The Arrow Slit

I clear the cobwebs from the slit.
The archer aims, draws back his bow
and lets the arrow fly.

It doesn't matter that eight hundred years
divides us from the air
sliced open by the arrowhead,

the archer tensed and quivering,
his target fixed, already dead
in the sharp mind of his eye –

a mind defined in action as he sees
the new ghost he has made.
All that matters is the string pulled tight,

the narrow view, the upright sky,
our concentration as we trace
the flight and where it went.

Our movements are identical:
we wipe our foreheads, blink back sweat,
take in the birdsong

and the fleshed-out trees
which sudden death failed to displace
then duck back swiftly in the shade.

Harmonica

Listen: the sound that you can hear
arriving faint and distant
over the rooftops and the washing lines,
through open windows, under doors –
over the student in her hammock
who tilts her head and sways
in the almost-imperceptible breeze,
over the attics and the red-brick walls,
the terraces inclining into shade,
the pub yards baked and emptying
four thousand miles from Memphis
where the creeping Mississippi
deposits its own delta as it slides down to the sea
in the hour between sunset and the dark
when boys dive from the concrete rim
despite the warning sign;
as households stoop and listen to the news,
when cats are stirring under cars
and parks are locked and chained
and pensioners lean on their spades
in well-kept gardens dried out in the heat
and the murmur of it travels to your ear
across the hinterland that lies between,
the patchy fields and new estates
with rail-lines cracking, unrepaired
and babies wake up for another feed
and watered plants exhale
in the never-to-be-repeated oneness
of an unremembered afternoon
unfolding, intersecting, holding back
its final shush of stillness before rain
while England pauses, counts her dead
is Ian as he cups his hand and plays.

Harlech and Beyond

That's what my ticket said.
On an exposed platform
in the fading autumn light
I stood there for a moment
where the coastal train divides.
No one to talk to or to ask.
Only the marshes and the dunes;
a distant farmhouse flickering.
Back then you needed to be sure
which carriage you were in:

one veered northwards
where the mountains reared;
the other headed south –
a wide arc following
the broad sweep of the bay,
the route that the invaders took
when England conquered Wales.
And so I took a risk,
trusting to luck and circumstance
to guide me to the place

where I should be.
Of course I took the right one
as if the future and the past
had entered into some unwritten bond,
leaving on the platform
a life lived differently
as the train with all the unsaid words
rattled through the night
between the mountains and the sea
to Harlech and beyond.

The Tango

When Valentino danced it on the silent silver screen
the women swooned and fainted in the aisles.
The thin-lipped mouth, the black and darting eyes,
the stamping boots and waistcoat of a Latin matador

proved too much for the unsuspecting wives
accustomed to the fox-trot, the cha-cha and the waltz
who drank poison by the hundred, slashed their wrists
or jumped from Brooklyn Bridge, the Empire State

finding life was not worth living when he died.
So clench the reddest rose between your teeth
and curl a sheer black calf around my thigh.
I'll march you up and down the parquet floor,

the band blindfolded in a room of potted palms.
Surrender to a passion you know can't be denied
and dance the tango – it takes two –
the dance of love, the dance of suicide.

House of Cards

She draws the curtains, pours the wine,
shuts out the demonstration in the street –

the sound of stragglers going home.
Instead she builds a house of cards,

cuts the deck and shuffles it
then deals them out as if she means to play:

a fragile compromise of hearts and kings
poised at the moment of its own collapse.

She hears it as a rumble under ice,
a necklace as it hits the floor and breaks,

the tingle spreading from her fingertips.
Her concentration holds it all in place,

the apex almost touching, quivering.
The slightest breath will bring it down.

Shakespeare's Lovers

Shakespeare's lovers lean into the light.
It's dawn, the birds are singing and the sun
is interrupting their shared dreams.
It takes purchase on the windowsills
and throws a woven pattern on the bed.
His villains linger in the shade –

the dark recesses of the mind
where nothing is the way it seems.
They want the darkness to extend
into the newborn day. More eloquent
than lovers they exhale the whole of night's
exhilarating air. The lovers wake and part.

His villains live to make their plots come true:
the maiden raped, the king stabbed in his sleep,
the trust of friends disrupted, undermined.
His lovers have no interest in
who lies to whom, who wears the crown.
They die before their love has chance to fade.

New Year

I won't go out. I'll watch the darkness spread
    all over England as the night takes hold.
From here the stars look hard, disinterested –
    sharp points of light against the purple sky.

So come in from the winter cold
    as one year breathes new life into the next.
In empty city office blocks, apartments
    built to house the new-made rich,

in small encampments everywhere
    people reclaim and occupy.
Downstairs the unwashed glassed cloud
    while bankers – nameless, out of reach –

and those who took us blindly into war
    toast the new year in with chilled champaigne,
the nation parcelled up and sold.
    We'll talk music, love, and politics,

predict the outcome of the latest push,
    the fall of kings, the likelihood of snow
and after midnight go to bed, the state
    a broken streetlamp that no-one wants to fix.

Metro

Hungry in Paris at eighteen
I searched my pockets, scrounged the fare
and took the Metro to Montmartre.
My first time on the underground:

a rush of hot escaping air,
posters peeling from the green-tiled walls,
the faces strained, anonymous,
a platform clock repeating its loud tick

to measure out the beating of my heart.
I had no language to express
the sudden surge of loneliness
that met me as I climbed the steps

into an open, floodlit square
where street girls selling roses danced,
the word *republic* whispered everywhere –
a tracking shot I moved through silently.

Last night I turned a corner, found
myself still waiting there
among the lovers and arcades
with empty pockets, empty hands –

an underworld of steel and rails
alive somewhere beneath my feet
before the last train swerved into the light,
before the doors slid shut on me.

Iron Hague

I take his leather gloves down from the wall.
    He hung them there after his final fight
    in Paris where he punched a man so hard
    he hit the deck and didn't rise again.
He swore he'd never go back in the ring

and never did. He found a pub in Mexborough,
    settled down; grew soft and fat and in the window seat
    watched trams and couples come and go –
    the blazers and straw hats and parasols,
an innocence that ended on the Somme:

the killing fields of Ypres and Bapaume.
    And there he learned to live a life
    outlasting its main purpose, every day the same
    and the man he'd floored looking up at him
from the bottom of each glass.

He'd earned his reputation and his name,
    trained in the yard of the Montagu Arms
    in a ring made from stacked beer crates,
    no punch bag but a door hung up in chains.
Collier's kiss-curl, shaven head, bare knuckles

on a Friday night, fighting for coppers thrown.
    His daughters knew my grandfather,
    threw him out at closing time –
    wore caps and braces, out-drank all the men.
We looked in through the glass to stare at them.

The town forgets its only claim to fame.
    A green plaque fades against the whitewashed wall.
    I walk down shuttered Main Street in the rain.
    A last drunk shadow-boxes his way
from lamp-post to lamp-post to home.

Cable Street

And this, my friend, is Cable Street.
Not much to look at I confess.
But this is where we took a final smoke
before we went to beat the Blackshirts down;

and this is where we drank a tepid pint
before we went to stop them in their tracks.
Why did I do it? I don't know.
Something to do with what the others did –

a thing to be lived not understood.
But when the mounted coppers came
to smash through our disputed barricade
I was the first to prise a cobble from the road

and couldn't help but wonder where they stood.
There's a scar on my forehead and here on my wrist.
You ought to take a leaf out of our book.
The whole East end lay open

but we wouldn't let them pass;
a hard-fought battle not to be forgot.
Here's a thing I picked up on the day.
I found it on the pavement, brought it home,

my waistcoat drenched into someone else's blood.
It's scuffed and bent and dented, out of shape;
The shine's gone off it and the glass is shot.
It still ticks if you tap it. Look.

Learning the Blues

I dreamt that I could play the blues.
The riffs came easy, effortless.
I coaxed the squirrels from the trees,
the Creole woman in her homespun dress.
I bent the notes and improvised.

The alligators surfaced for a while
then sank back sleeping, satisfied
and harmless in the sluggish riverbed.
Howling Wolf was waiting in the queue.
The bayous emptied,

girls kicked off their shoes.
The back porch creaked under my tread.
The dream imparted confidence I guess.
Next day I rummaged in the drawer
and there among the usual stuff –

the cellotape and rubber bands
I found the old harmonica
my grandfather had brought back
from the war. I tapped it
on my open palm and blew.

My confidence was misplaced.
The notes came thin and dusty
but there was something shimmering
below the surface of the tune.
I practiced the one lick for days

then went to the old bluesman for advice.
He lived along the waterfront
as all old bluesmen do.
Surrounded by his forty-fives
he sipped Jack Daniels over ice.

He was sparing in his praise.
I played. He listened. *Son* he said
soak your harp in bourbon overnight.
You won't sound any better
but man just think of the taste.

Chantry Bridge

We sit together in the window seat
to watch the swollen river slide
over the sharp edge of the weir.

A week of rain has drained the upland farms,
depositing its random debris here –
a huge black tyre, a barbed-wire fence,

the branches of a splintered tree
banked up against the man-made island where
grey grass blows back and willows bend,

a tuft of land the waters inundate.
The traffic slows and stops to hide
the ornamental chantry on the bridge

where Clifford struck young Rutland down
despite his pleas for mercy or his age.
His hot blood swirls and eddies at our feet.

When I reach out to take you in my arms
there is no present, past, or future tense –
only the moment and the river poised

forever on the endless brink
before it dips and takes itself away
to flow and flow and end in turbulence.

Queen's Square

That strange lull between Christmas
and the start of the New Year
when nothing ever happens except rain.

Head down I cut across the square –
the Black Prince pointing from his horse,
his torso awkward, swivelling

with water streaming from his armoured back.
On the platform, counting down
my last train stood, about to leave.

Coloured lights strung the periphery
or hung suspended from the massive tree.
I felt a tugging at my sleeve

and saw a ragged, half-familiar face
under the lights, pressed close, the sack
of some grey cowl around his neck

but fading quickly into the crowd
like someone sinking in the sea
wide-eyed and looking up to find some hope

but finding none and letting go,
holding on just long enough
to say *Don't you remember me?*

Bloody Meadows

White flurries round the hawthorn tree.
A bridge of bodies spans the icy beck –
a hundred thousand arrows shot

and sprouting from the ground.
Drenched pinions hanging limp,
The quartered liveries. A blizzard

shutting out the fading sun,
the splayed and naked bodies of the dead.
The grave-pits gaping

and the north wind merciless,
the killing fields below;
the chaotic roar subsiding

where they poured over the ledge –
the sudden dip, the steep incline,
lost footing, clutching hands,

the long and ragged rout.
A road of bodies through the April drifts.
A twist of frozen breath.

And in Lead chapel vespers sung.
The abandoned debris of the battlefield.
Blood melting virgin snow, The hand of God.

Ice

Some say the universe will end in fire:
a final conflagration burning up
the world and all that's in it.

But walking out there with my son,
crossing the moors in need of sleep –
lost when the sun gave way to the moon

and the moon itself reflected
in frozen puddles fractured by our tread –
I knew there was a stark alternative:

that cold and overtaking snow
might cover and obliterate our cities and our towns
as surely as it covered up our footsteps as we trod

our flagging circuit, climbed a final hill
and dropped into a valley off the map,
deep-drifted between dry-stone walls.

There we found shelter, lit a lamp,
broke bread together, drank our fill and slept.
The heat was meagre but it was enough.

The memory flickers but it will suffice.
Since then my son has slipped and gone
into a fissure deep and wide,

a sheer transparent precipice
from which there'll be no clambering.
Now I believe the world will end in ice.

Elegy for the Chartist Poets

for Ray Hearne

1

There will be silence after all these deaths:
the unrelenting sun will turn to stone,

the clocks will strike a final time then stop,
the drunks will sink a last pint and go home

down streets where a few cobbles still survive,
through squares and alleys riddled with the past.

The books will close forever on the page
in libraries whose shelves are thick with dust.

While up there on the long extended ridge
where winter tears the topsoil from the rock

and twists the trees into the shapes of souls
or in the valley bottom where the stream

ran fast to spin the ever-turning wheel
a voice will challenge silence then go still;

the sleeping lovers wake up from their dream
and fall to listening in the ghost-grey dawn.

2

This is the sharp edge of the north – the place
to which the quivering needle points, the root

and source of our resistance and dissent.
The wind has taken everything away:

the pamphlet and the broadsheet and the poem,
snatched them down from the windowsills and walls

and sent them in a spiral through the air –
charred fragments carried upwards to ignite

then come to rest under our waiting feet.
They flare there for a moment then subside.

I saw a vision on the Sabbath Day:
a huge avenging angel with red wings

alighted on the top of Blackstone Edge
and, like the sentinel he was, looked round

on towns and cities spread out on the plain,
the cursed, devoted landscape shuddering.

His feet were rooted to the solid earth,
his head was in the sky. A thunderstorm

was heaving in the west, rain clouds opened
and poured down into the gaping mouths

of great crowds gathered on the plains below.
They came barefooted and in need of bread;

they came under the banners arm in arm,
leaving the workshops empty in the dawn,

the rich mill owners turning in their beds.
They paid a penny for *The Northern Star*,

hunched round a single candle in the gloom
and read it to each other with wide eyes.

The poets printed liberty on each
and every page, on each and every eye.

Outside the world of commerce chimed and whirred,
the factories hummed and ticked, the coins fell ripe

and golden in the hands of guilty men
while children hauled the coal-tubs underground.

I call them out of darkness with their words:
the incantations of the working poor -

the language of the lost and dispossessed:
the mill-hands, miners, labourers in the field,

the muffled voices straining to be heard.
The incremental stirrings in the dust.

3

The places where it happened still survive:
a trace of it outlives them in the air

at Newport where the redcoats shot them down
or Sheffield where the chimneys and the soot

had crammed them into tenements to die.
Holberry raising hell up from the streets,

placing his weapons in the empty hands
of ragged boys and crude intemperate men

and giving them a date and time and place
to turn the tables over, stop the clocks.

A first incursion, arrests at midnight;
men dragged from houses leaving screaming wives.

Holberry picking hemp inside York gaol,
his fingers bleeding as he prised it free,

unravelling his past with every thread.
Ten thousand mourners when his funeral

twisted through the tangled alleyways
finding no resolution and no rest.

*From Hull and Halifax and Hell good Lord
deliver me.* The infant at the breast.

4

I must have caught the dying breath of it
when I was still a child: the furnace doors

wide open and the sleek, bare-chested men
pouring the liquid metal into moulds.

I saw it from the window of a train;
heard loud insistent hammers beating out

a rhythm as they forged the man-made chains.
And there, over the dark horizon's rim

the steel city's furnaces puthering:
a column of tall dust throughout the day,

a pillar of fire glowing in the night.
Hymns swelling from the chapel on the hill,

torches, marches, gatherings, illicit
meetings under the beams of hidden pubs.

It's in the faded photograph I saw
of two old Chartists posing with their pikes,

their faces weathered and their wrinkled eyes
fixed on the future, resolute, despite

the years of trampling and the failing cries.
Or go to Darfield churchyard in a mist

and find out where the Corn-Law Rhymer lies -
his gravestone overlooking fields of corn,

the railings round his tombstone flaking rust.
How Byron snubbed him, turned his lordly back

on Elliott and his kind, refused to speak
or recognise a man whose hands had toiled.

Or Ernest Jones inside his threadbare cell,
scratching his poems in blood across the page

because the living ink had been denied.
I hold his fragile papers to the light,

feel his stained fingers on the nib
and hear the secret scratching of his pen.

Lift me up and put me down, set me free
on some high, open point where I can see

the whole of the broke past entire, the stunned
and ravaged landscape spread out under me.

5

Mad Shelley dreamt it and the dream survived.
A flicker in the corner of his eye

burned through his death and went on to ignite
a hungry generation with its spark.

The Chartist poets whisper in my ear:
Don't let us be forgotten. Set us free.

We lie in the cold earth till Judgement Day
scourges the valley bottom with its fire.

Our ink is dry. Our mouths are filled with clay.
Our ears are stopped to what is said above.

The purple clouds are riven and we rise.
So keep your lines uncluttered, bold, and clear;

stake out the untilled region of the heart
and let it thrive. Restore us to the light.

The gagged and muted people found a voice:
it rose up from the cuttings and the seams

and gathered its momentum from the crowd.
What remains? The dignity of labour

is a lie. We sweated for our children
and they died. We met and marched together

on parliament, were turned away ignored -
our petitions, our grievances unread.

Where can we turn to now for our redress?
They want to keep you ignorant of us;

they want our voices buried underneath
a layer of history so we can't be heard.

We rise up from our tombs and agitate.
We knock here now until you let us in.

These are our true fathers, our true mothers,
our true friends, our lost progenitors

who ask across the intervening years
the untenable question *What remains?*

Smoke drifts across the furrows and the fields;
the moon already has a reddish cast.

6

Snow falling from God's heaven black with soot,
the Calder Valley thick with it, the ice

sheeting the hillsides where they pulled and climbed.
A few flakes dance and settle on my tongue.

In Manchester, in Sheffield, and in Leeds -
in all the places where their mark was left

the statues of the undeserving rich
gaze down impervious from their stone-hewn plinths.

The traffic slides and judders to a halt
where shopping centres interrupt the flow

of what we were and are or might still be.
Your songs preserve the bite and spleen of it

and when you sing them without compromise
the voices of the dead who sang before

join in to swell the chorus of your song.
Now rain comes on in huge, successive waves.

It washes guiltless blood from cobblestones.
It rinses teardrops from the chiselled eye.

It runs unhindered down the workhouse walls.
The doors are barred, the candles have gone out,

the presses fallen silent. A cold ghost
repeats their spare, hard verses where they trod.

Out where the moors are brittle, blackened, burned
and silence levels everything with night;

out there under the grey indifferent sky
the Chartist poets lie in unmarked graves.

Acknowledgements

Thanks are due to the editors of the following in which some of these poems first appeared: *Critical Survey, Dream Catcher, Endymion, English Chicago Review, Horizon Review, Lampeter Review, London Magazine, The Morning Star, New Walk Magazine, The Slab, Structo, The Times Literary Supplement, Trespass Magazine, Turbulence, Westminster Review;* Ross Bradshaw (ed) *Maps,* Shane Rhodes (ed) *10 Miles East of England,* Andy Jackson (ed) *Double Bill,* Oz Hardwick and Miles Salter (eds) *The Valley Press Anthology of Yorkshire Poetry,* Dan Ryder (curator) *These poets our kin/These poems our stories* (exhibition at Frenchgate Centre, Doncaster) and Angela Topping (ed) *Shakespeare Poems.* A number of these poems were written during a residency at Gladstone's Library in 2012. Acknowledgements are also due to the Janice Long Spoken Word Sessions, BBC Radio 2. Thanks the Royal Literary Fund for assistance during the writing of this collection.